W9-ARU-127

A Busy Guy

By Charnan Simon

Illustrated by
Joan Holub

Rookie reader®

Children's Press®
A Division of Scholastic Inc.
New York Toronto London Auckland Sydney
Mexico City New Delhi Hong Kong
Danbury, Connecticut

For the real Daniel Robinson, and for Michael, Andy, and Joel, busy guys all.
—C. S.

For Jay, Debbie, and Holland Gallagher
—J. H.

Reading Consultant
Linda Cornwell
Learning Resource Consultant
Indiana Department of Education

Library of Congress Cataloging-in-Publication Data
Simon, Charnan.
A busy guy / by Charnan Simon ; illustrated by Joan Holub.
p. cm. — (Rookie reader)
Summary: Daniel is busy on every day of the week, painting the toolshed on Monday, fixing his sister's bike on Tuesday, finding himself more mischievous than helpful by Saturday, and resting on Sunday.
ISBN 0-516-20396-7
[1. Days—Fiction.] I. Holub, Joan, ill. II. Title. III. Series.
PZ7.S6035Bu 1997
[E] —DC21

96-49442
CIP
AC

Daniel Robinson was a busy guy.

On Monday,
he planted a garden for his mother . . .

. . . and painted the toolshed
for his father.

7

On Tuesday, he fixed up his bike,

then went to work on his big sister's.

On Wednesday,
Daniel gave the dog a haircut . . .

14

. . . and a bath.

On Thursday morning,
he operated on his little sister's sick doll.

17

Thursday afternoon,
Daniel had to go shopping.

On Friday,
Daniel's friends came over to build a fort . . .

. . . and fish in the creek.

On Saturday,
Daniel made breakfast for his whole family,

then got to eat a second breakfast at the Pancake House.

On Sunday, Daniel rested.

Tomorrow would be another busy day.

Word List (72 words)

a	Daniel's	go	operated	Thursday
afternoon	day	got	over	to
and	dog	guy	painted	tomorrow
another	doll	had	Pancake	toolshed
at	eat	haircut	planted	Tuesday
bath	family	he	rested	up
be	father	his	Robinson	was
big	fish	House	Saturday	Wednesday
bike	fixed	in	second	went
breakfast	for	little	shopping	whole
build	fort	made	sick	work
busy	Friday	Monday	sister's	would
came	friends	morning	Sunday	
creek	garden	mother	the	
Daniel	gave	on	then	

About the Author

Charnan Simon lives in Madison, Wisconsin, with her husband, Tom Kazunas, and her daughters, Ariel and Hana. Charnan spends her time reading and writing books and keeping up with her very busy family. Other Rookie Readers by Charnan Simon include *Sam and Dasher* and *Come! Sit! Speak!*

About the Illustrator

Joan Holub has written five children's books including *Pen Pals* and *Boo Who?* and has illustrated many other books. She used watercolor and ink to make the illustrations for *A Busy Guy.*